MAX on life
cd-book :: study

Dealing with Difficult People

4 Interactive Bible Studies
for Individuals or Small Groups

MAX LUCADO

THOMAS NELSON PUBLISHERS

Published by Thomas Nelson, Inc., P.O. Box 141000, Nashville, Tennessee, 37214.
Study Guide prepared by the Specialty Group of Thomas Nelson, Inc.
Excerpts are from *Facing Your Giants, God Came Near, In the Grip of Grace,* and
No Wonder They Call Him the Savior, published by W Publishing Group. Used by permission.

ISBN -10: 1404104887
ISBN -13: 9781404104884

Printed and bound in the United States of America

www.thomasnelson.com

CONTENTS

HOW TO USE THIS STUDY GUIDE

Congratulations! You are making God's Word a priority. These moments of reflection will change you forever. Here are a few suggestions for you to get the most out of your individual study.

1

As you begin each study, pray that God will speak to you through his Word.

2

Read the overview to each study, then listen to the audio segment, taking notes on the worksheet provided.

3

Following the audio segment, respond to the personal Bible study and reflection questions. These questions are designed to take you deeper into God's Word and help you focus on God and on the theme of the study.

4

There are three types of questions used in the study. *Observation* questions focus on the basic facts: who, what, when, where, and how. *Interpretation* questions delve into the meaning of the passage. *Application* questions help you get practical: discovering the implications of the text for growing in Christ. These three keys will help you unlock the treasures of Scripture.

5

Write your answers to the questions in the spaces provided or in a personal journal. Writing brings clarity and deeper understanding of yourself and of God's Word.

6

Keep a Bible dictionary handy. Use it to look up any unfamiliar words, names, or places.

7

Have fun! Studying God's Word can bring tremendous rewards to your life. Allow the Holy Spirit to illuminate your mind to the amazing applications each study can have in your daily life. ■

INTRODUCTION

DEALING WITH DIFFICULT PEOPLE

Heaven knows you could use some inspiration. People can exhaust you. And there are times when all we can do is not enough. I don't, for a moment, intend to minimize the challenges some of you face. You're tired. You're angry. You're disappointed.

May I urge you to do all you can to see people as God sees them? Why should you? So you can understand the depth of God's love.

When you love the unloving, you get a glimpse of what God does for you. When you keep the porch light on for the prodigal child, when you do what is right even though you have been done wrong, when you love the weak and the sick, you do what God does every single moment. Covenant-keeping enrolls you in the post-graduate school of God's love.

Is this why God has given you this challenge? When you love liars, cheaters, and heartbreakers, are you not doing what God has done for us? Pay attention to and take notes on your struggles. God invites you to understand his love.

He also wants you to illustrate it.

David did with Mephibosheth. David was a walking parable of God's loyalty. Hosea did the same with Gomer. He wardrobed divine devotion. God calls you to do the same. Illustrate stubborn love. God is giving you a Mephibosheth-size chance to show your children and your neighbors what real love does.

Embrace it. Who knows? Someone may tell your story of loyalty to illustrate the loyalty of God. ■

See your enemies, not as God's failures, but as God's projects.

Max Lucado

LESSON ONE:

THE RIGHT WAY TO SEE PEOPLE

Do to others what you want them to do to you.

MATTHEW 7:12

OVERVIEW

On any other day, I probably wouldn't have stopped. Like the majority of people on the busy avenue, I would hardly have noticed him standing there. But the very thing on my mind was the very reason he was there, so I stopped.

I'd just spent a portion of the morning preparing a lesson out of the ninth chapter of John, the chapter that contains the story about the man blind from birth. I'd finished lunch and was returning to my office when I saw him. He was singing. An aluminum cane was in his left hand; his right hand was extended and open, awaiting donations. He was blind.

After walking past him about five steps, I stopped and mumbled something to myself about the epitome of hypocrisy and went back in his direction. I put some change in his hand. "Thank you," he said and then offered me a common Brazilian salutation, "and may you have health." Ironic wish.

Once again I started on my way. Once again the morning study of John 9 stopped me. "Jesus saw a man, blind from birth." I paused and pondered. If Jesus were here he would *see* this man. I wasn't sure what that meant. But I was sure I hadn't done it. So I turned around again.

As if the giving of a donation entitled me to do so, I stopped beside a nearby car and observed. I challenged myself to see him. I would stay here until I saw more than a sightless indigent on a busy thoroughfare in downtown Rio de Janeiro.

I watched him sing. He stood tall. And he sang. Loudly. Even proudly. All of us had more reason to sing than he, but he was the one singing. He was singing from contentment. Somehow this eyeless pauper had discovered a candle called satisfaction and it glowed in his dark world. Someone had told him, or maybe he'd told himself, that tomorrow's joy is fathered by today's acceptance.

Though the man I now saw was still sightless, he was remarkably insightful. And though I was the one with eyes, it was he who gave me a new vision.

PART 1: FOLLOW-ALONG NOTES

USE THIS WORKSHEET AS YOU LISTEN TO "DEALING WITH DIFFICULT PEOPLE, PART 1."

- John 9:1-21

- Jesus didn't see a handicapped person, he saw a person with a handicap.

THREE WAYS OF SEEING THE MAN BORN BLIND

1. Followers of Jesus saw a ______________________________. John 9:2

2. The neighbors saw a ______________________________. John 9:8

Labeling is an easy way to ______________________________.

Labeling is drawing a conclusion before __________________________________.

Labeling is the lazy effort of determining the ______________________________

____.

Two reasons people are not so easily labeled:

1.

2.

3. The parents were ____. John 9:18-21

- The reason the man was born blind ______________________________________

  ____.

- The blind man was thrown out ____

  ____.

PART 2: GOING DEEPER

PERSONAL STUDY AND REFLECTION

- Do you tend to see the person or the problem they possess first? List steps you can take to see people first.

- We are all guilty of applying labels to people. Share some ways to avoid this practice.

____

____

____

____

____

____

- Don't ______________ other people, and you will not be ______________.

  Don't __________________ others of being guilty, and you will not be

  ______________ of being ______________. Forgive, and ______________

  will be ______________. Luke 6:37

- Jesus often reached out to the outcast of society. Share some ministry ideas to follow this pattern.

- *Jesus didn't see a blind man. He saw a man born blind. Jesus demonstrated the work of God.*

- What fears do you face in attempting to reach out to those with such great needs?

____

____

____

____

- List in your own words "the right way to live" given in Titus 3:1-2.

____

____

____

____

____

- The followers of Christ saw many miracles. Why were they so caught up in the cause of the blindness instead of the reason for the healing?

____

____

____

____

____

Matching:

_____ Be humble	1. Colossians 4:6
_____ Speak truth in love	2. 1 Peter 5:6
_____ Don't depend on human wisdom	3. Ephesians 4:15
_____ Speak kind and pleasant	4. 1 Corinthians 2:5

- **Read Corinthians 12:7-10.** Why was Paul given the thorn in the flesh? How did he use it for good?

- **Read Matthew 7:1-2.** Consider the serious message of this verse. How should we live in light of this verse?

A loving heart is the truest wisdom.

CHARLES DICKENS

LESSON TWO:

WHEN YOU AND YOUR KIN CAN'T GET ALONG

Good people will be happy in the LORD
and will find protection in Him.

PSALM 64:10

OVERVIEW

Forgiveness is not foolish.

Forgiveness is, at its core, choosing to see your offender with different eyes. When some Moravian missionaries took the message of God to the Eskimos, the missionaries struggled to find a word in the native language for forgiveness. The finally landed on this cumbersome twenty-four-letter choice: *issumagijoujungnainermik.* This formidable assembly of letters is literally translated "not being able to think about it anymore."

To forgive is to move on, not to think about the offense anymore. You don't excuse him, endorse her, or embrace them. You just route thoughts about them through heaven. You see the one who causes hurt as God's child and revenge as God's job.

By the way, how can we grace-recipients do anything less? Dare we ask God for grace when we refuse to give it? This is a huge issue in Scripture. Jesus was tough on sinners who refused to forgive other sinners. Remember the story about the servant in Matthew 18. He stirred the wrath of God: "You evil servant! Because you begged me to forget what you owed, I told you that you did not have to pay anything. You should have showed mercy to that other servant, just as I showed mercy to you" (Matthew 18:32-33).

In the final sum, we give grace because we've been given grace. We survive because we imitate the Survivor Tree. We reach our roots beyond the bomb zone. We tap into moisture beyond the explosion. We dig deeper and deeper until we draw moisture from the mercy of God.

We have been given grace. We can freely give it even to our earthly family who has caused hurt and pain in our lives. ✎

PART 1: FOLLOW-ALONG NOTES

USE THIS WORKSHEET AS YOU LISTEN TO "DEALING WITH DIFFICULT PEOPLE, PART 2."

WHY IT HURTS WHEN LIFE IS *RELATIVELY* DIFFICULT

Family can be ______________________________ to our hurts. (closed eyes)

Family can be _______________________ when they speak. (hateful tongue)

The closer the ____________, the more painful the _____________________.

Family can be ___________________________ when they act. (poking noses)

Family can be ____________________________ in their support. (cold heart)

PROBLEMS IN THE FAMILY OF JESUS

Mark 6:3

Matthew 13:27

Luke 4:16, 29, 30

Mark 3:21

HOW TO COPE

1. ______________________________ your blessing

Matthew 4:17

Galatians 4:6

2. ______________________________ your family

Mark 3:35

3. ______________________________ your expectations

Luke 21:16

4. ______________________________ your judgment

1 Corinthians 15:3-7

Acts 1:14

Galatians 1:18-19

PART 2:
GOING DEEPER

PERSONAL STUDY AND REFLECTION

- You can't control how people will respond to you. As you think about that statement, what attitude within yourself needs to change?

- Which characteristic of an unsupportive family member is most difficult for you?

- **Read Mark 3:20-35.** Describe how Jesus responded to his family.

- Are you surprised by the way Jesus was treated by his family? What surprises you the most?

- List the ways you will implement coping methods in your attempt to handle difficult family relationships.

Begin to list specific prayer requests for the person in your family who is most difficult. Make an effort to pray for those needs.

___

___

___

___

___

___

___

- But I say to you, ___ your ___.

  ___ for those who ___ you.

  Matthew 5:44 ■

It requires less character
to discover the faults of others
than it does to tolerate them.

J. Petit-Senn

LESSON THREE:

KEEPING THE PEACE IN GOD'S FAMILY

Salt is good, . . . so, be full of salt, and have peace with each other.

MARK 9:50

OVERVIEW

God has enlisted us in his navy and placed us on his ship. The boat has one purpose—to carry us safely to the other shore.

This is no cruise ship; it's a battleship. We aren't called to a life of leisure; we are called to a life of service. Each of us has a different task. Some, concerned with those who are drowning, are snatching people from the water. Others are occupied with the enemy, so they man the cannons of prayer and worship. Still others, devote themselves to the crew, feeding and training the crew members.

Though different, we are the same. Each can tell of a personal encounter with the Captain, for each has received a personal call. He found us among the shanties of the seaport and invited us to follow him. Our faith was born at the sight of his fondness, and so we went.

We each followed him across the gangplank of his grace onto the same boat. There is one captain and one destination. Though the battle is fierce, the boat is safe, for our captain is God. The ship will not sink. For that, there is no concern.

There is concern, however, regarding the disharmony of the crew. When we first boarded we assumed the crew was made up of others like us. But as we've wandered these decks, we've encountered curious converts with curious appearances. Some wear uniforms we've never seen, sporting styles we've never witnessed. The variety of dress is not nearly as disturbing as the plethora of opinions.

Some think once you're on the boat, you can't get off. Others say you'd be foolish to go overboard, but the choice is yours.

Some believe you volunteer for service; others believe you were destined for the service before the ship was even built.

There are those who speak to the captain in a personal language. There are those who think such languages are extinct.

Oh, how we tend to cluster.

The consequence is a rocky boat. There is trouble on deck. Fights have broken out. Sailors have refused to speak to each other. There have even been times when one group refused to acknowledge the presence of others on the ship. Most tragically, some adrift at sea have chosen not to board the boat because of the quarreling of the sailors.

"What do we do?" we'd like to ask the Captain. "How can there be harmony on the ship?" We don't have to go far to find the answer.

On the last night of his life Jesus prayed a prayer that stands as a citadel for all Christians:

"I pray for these followers, but I am also praying for all those who will believe in me because of their teaching. Father, I pray that they can be one. As you are in me and I am in you, I pray that they can also be one in us. Then the world will believe that you sent me" (John 17:20-21).

How precious are these words. Jesus, knowing the end is near, prays one final time for his followers. Striking, isn't it, that he prayed not for their success, their safety, or their happiness. He prayed for their unity. He prayed that they would love each other.

As he prayed for them, he also prayed for "those who will believe because of their teaching." That means us! In his last prayer Jesus prayed that you and I be one. ✎

PART 1:
FOLLOW-ALONG NOTES

USE THIS WORKSHEET AS YOU LISTEN TO "DEALING WITH DIFFICULT PEOPLE, PART 3."

PROBLEMS IN CAPERNAUM

Mark 9:33-38

The Problem: ______________________________

Mark 9:33

James 3:16

The Solution: ______________________________

Mark 9:37

The Question from John:____

Mark 9:38

Ways to discern: ____

____

John 17:39-40

Unity ____ to God.

Prayer of Christ

John 17:20

Unity ____ belief.

PART 2:
GOING DEEPER

PERSONAL STUDY AND REFLECTION

- We are called to a life of service, and each of us has a different task. What is the specific task to which God has called you? How are you serving God on the "ship?"

- As you honestly look at your own life, would you say you have more often helped to keep unity or to create disunity in the family of God?

- *Jesus teaches that acceptance is the answer to arguments.*

- Give an example of hard lessons learned through seeing the results of disunity in a body of believers.

____

____

____

____

____

____

____

____

- It is ________________ and ________________ when God's people live together in ___________________. Psalm 133:1

- We are not told to "build" unity. We are told to "keep" unity. In your own words, describe the difference.

- *Jesus was a source of unity. He was literally an oasis of cooperation in the middle of a desert of division.*

Whoever accepts a child like this in my name accepts me. And whoever accepts me accepts the One who sent me.

Mark 9:37

- Acceptance is the first step to unity. What is the difference between acceptance and agreement?

____

____

____

____

____

____

____

____

- Just because a group is feeding the hungry or providing clothes to the poor does not mean they are Christians. Jesus doesn't issue a call for blind tolerance. Why is discernment an important part of unity?

- List qualities you look for in a good ministry.

- **Read Ephesians 4:3-7.** What command is given in verse 3? How is this to be accomplished?

It is as easy to draw back a stone,
thrown with force from the hand,
as to recall a word once spoken.

MENANDER

LESSON FOUR:

DIFFICULT PEOPLE ARE GOD'S PRIORITY

The LORD says, "I made myself known to people who were not looking for me."

Isaiah 65:1

OVERVIEW

Value is measured by two criteria, appearance and performance. Pretty tough system, isn't it? Where does that leave the retarded? Or the ugly or uneducated? Where does that place the aged or the handicapped? What hope does that offer the unborn child? Not much. Not much at all. We become nameless numbers on mislaid lists.

Now please understand, this is man's value system. It is not God's. His plan is much brighter. God, with eyes twinkling, steps up to the philosopher's blackboard, erases the never-ending, ever-repeating circle of history and replaces it with a line; a hopefilled, promising, slender line. And, looking over his shoulder to see if the class is watching, he draws an arrow on the end.

In God's book man is heading somewhere. He has an amazing destiny. We are being prepared to walk down the church aisle and become the bride of Jesus. We are going to live with him. Share the throne with him. We count. We are valuable. And what's more, our worth is built in! Our value is inborn.

You see, if there was anything that Jesus wanted everyone to understand it was this: A person is worth something simply because he is a person. That is why he treated people like he did.

Listen closely. Jesus' love does not depend upon what we do for him. Not at all. In the eyes of the King, you have value simply because you are. You don't have to look nice or perform well. Your value is inborn.

Period.

Think about that for just a minute. You are valuable just because you exist. Not because of what you do or what you have done, but simply because you are. Remember that. Remember that the next time you are left bobbing in the wake of someone's steamboat ambition. Remember that the next time some trickster tries to hang a bargain basement price tag on your self-worth. The next time someone tries to pass you off as a cheap buy, just think about the way Jesus honors you . . . and smile.

I do. I smile because I know I don't deserve love like that. None of us does.

PART 1: FOLLOW-ALONG NOTES

USE THIS WORKSHEET AS YOU LISTEN TO "DEALING WITH DIFFICULT PEOPLE, PART 4."

2 Corinthians 5:16

This verse should change: ____

____

Jesus saw Matthew in a different light - Luke 9:27-28

Jesus saw ____.

Jesus want us to see ____.

Is the light on in your world? It is if you are plugged into ______________.

The response of Matthew – Luke 9:29

Matthew had a ______________________________ for Jesus and his friends.

The entrance of the religious heat – Luke 9:30-31

The Pharisees ____________________ Jesus for eating and drinking with a tax collector.

This is an encounter between the priority of God and ___________________.

Matthew had two things that the Pharisees did not have:

____

____

PART 2: GOING DEEPER

PERSONAL STUDY AND REFLECTION

- Have you ever thought of Matthew as an unlikely follower? List any other Bible characters you have viewed as unlikely followers of Christ?

___

___

___

___

___

___

___

- The people of that day were shocked at Jesus reaching out to Matthew. Have you been shocked at a church or pastor reaching out to someone in your community? Why?

____

____

____

____

____

____

____

____

- *There was something about the way Jesus thought of people that was diametrically opposed to the way everyone else thought about people.*

- The religious crowd of that day was offended by the actions of Jesus. Does this happen in religious circles today? What needs to be done to change those attitudes?

____

____

____

____

____

____

____

____

- *The challenge is to learn to see what Jesus can see in people.*

- As you read 2 Corinthians 5:16, what changes need to take place in your heart towards folks outside your circle of friends?

____

____

____

____

____

____

- Share why you feel the following were unlikely followers of Christ:

Saul ______________________________________

Zacchaeus __________________________________

Peter ______________________________________

- List some ministry ideas for the local church to reach out to others beyond their comfort zone.

PROMISES FROM DEALING WITH DIFFICULT PEOPLE

Savor the following promises that God gives to those who determine to deal with difficult people properly. One way that you can carry the message of this study with you everywhere in your heart is through the lost art of Scripture memorization. Select a few of the verses below to commit to memory.

Know that the LORD is God.
He made us, and we belong to him;
we are his people, the sheep he tends.

PSALM 100:3

Love never hurts a neighbor,
so loving is obeying all the law.

ROMANS 13:10

Good people care about justice for the poor,
but the wicked are not concerned.

PROVERBS 29:7

The LORD looked down from heaven on all people to see if anyone understood, if anyone was looking to God for help.

Psalm 14:2

And from far away the LORD appeared to his people and said, "I love you people with a love that will last forever. That is why I have continued showing you kindness."

Jeremiah 31:3

This is my command: Love each other as I have loved you. The greatest love a person can show is to die for his friends.

John 15:12-13

Keep on loving each other as brothers and sister. Remember to welcome strangers, because some who have done this have welcomed angels without knowing it.

Hebrews 13:1-2

The LORD is pleased with his people: he saves the humble.

Psalm 149:4

SUGGESTIONS FOR MEMBERS OF A GROUP STUDY

The Bible says that we should not forsake the assembling of ourselves together (see Hebrews 10:25). A small-group Bible study is one of the best ways to grow in your faith. As you meet together with other people, you will discover new truths about God's Word and challenge one another to greater levels of faith. The following are suggestions for you to get the most out of a small-group study of this material.

1. Come to the study prepared. Follow the suggestions for individual study mentioned previously. You will find that careful preparation will greatly enrich your time spent in group discussion.

2. Be willing to participate in the discussion. The leader of your group will not be lecturing. Instead, he or she will be encouraging the members of the group to discuss what they have learned. The leader will be asking the questions that are found in this guide.

3. Stick to the topic being discussed.

4. Be sensitive to the other members of the group. Listen attentively when they describe what they have learned. You may be surprised by their insights! Many questions do not have "right" answers, particularly questions that aim at meaning or application. Instead the questions push us to explore the passage more thoroughly.

5. When possible, link what you say to the comments of others. Also be affirming whenever you can. This will encourage some of the more hesitant members of the group to participate.

6. Expect God to teach you through the passage being discussed and through the other members of the group. Pray that you will have an enjoyable and profitable time together, but also that as a result of this study, you will find ways that you can take action individually and/or as a group.

7. Remember that anything said in the group is considered confidential and should not be discussed outside the group unless specific permission is given to do so.

LEADER'S GUIDE

LESSON ONE: THE RIGHT WAY TO SEE PEOPLE

1. Begin the session with prayer. Ask God to be with you as you begin to study his Word together.

2. Play the audio segment of the CD entitled "Dealing with Difficult People, Part 1." Encourage group members to take notes in the section of their study guide entitled "Follow-Along Notes."

3. Begin group discussion by asking the following questions. Allow each group member ample time to answer, if they desire to do so.

    - Think about your initial response to people and how it needs to reflect God's love. How would you improve your attitude?
    - Share problems with labeling people.
    - Do you find yourself disappointed in the response of the followers of Christ? What bothers you the most?
    - What attitude should the neighbors have toward this man with a handicap?

- Share reasons it is difficult to overcome the habit of labeling.

4. Remind everyone to complete the "Going Deeper: Personal Study and Reflection" section for lesson two before the next group session.

5. Be sure to close in prayer. Invite the group participants to share prayer requests with the group and encourage them to pray for one another.

LESSON TWO:
WHEN YOU AND YOUR KIN CAN'T GET ALONG

1. Begin the session with prayer. Ask God to be with you as you begin to study his Word together.

2. Play the audio segment of the CD entitled "Dealing with Difficult People, Part 2." Encourage group members to take notes in the section of their study guide entitled "Follow-Along Notes."

3. Begin group discussion by asking the following questions. Allow each group member ample time to answer, if they desire to do so.

- Why is it difficult to overcome disapproval from family members?
- How do you get beyond the hurts caused by family?
- Discuss the possible reasons that the family of Jesus did not believe.
- Give some practical ways to use the tools given to cope with difficult family.
- Share ways the church can compensate for difficult family relationships as your spiritual family.

4. Remind everyone to complete the "Going Deeper: Personal Study and Reflection" section for lesson three before the next group session.

5. Be sure to close in prayer. Invite the group participants to share prayer requests with the group and encourage them to pray for one another.

LESSON THREE: KEEPING THE PEACE IN GOD'S FAMILY

1. Begin the session with prayer. Ask God to be with you as you begin to study his Word together.

2. Play the audio segment of the CD entitled "Dealing with Difficult People, Part 3." Encourage group members to take notes in the section of their study guide entitled "Follow-Along Notes."

3. Begin group discussion by asking the following questions. Allow each group member ample time to answer, if they desire to do so.

    - Why do you think the church struggles with conflict?
    - What obstacles does such behavior create for ministry?
    - Share ways to keep unity in the church.
    - Acceptance begins the process of creating unity. Share other necessary steps in the process.

4. Remind everyone to complete the "Going Deeper: Personal Study and Reflection" section for lesson four before the next group session.

5. Be sure to close in prayer. Invite the group participants to share prayer requests with the group and encourage them to pray for one another.

LESSON FOUR:

DIFFICULT PEOPLE ARE GOD'S PRIORITY

1. Begin the session with prayer. Ask God to be with you as you begin to study his Word together.

2. Play the audio segment of the CD entitled "Dealing with Difficult People, Part 4." Encourage group members to take notes in the section of their study guide entitled "Follow-Along Notes."

3. Begin group discussion by asking the following questions. Allow each group member ample time to answer, if they desire to do so.
    - Do you know an unlikely follower of Christ? Perhaps you were such a person and wish to share your story.
    - Why do we tend to give up on various folks ever accepting Christ?
    - Share some ministry ideas to reach "Matthew" in your world.
    - Give some of the rewards that come from ministering to such folks.

4. Be sure to close in prayer. Invite the group participants to share prayer requests with the group and encourage them to pray for one another.

MAX LUCADO'S

MAX on life

SERIES

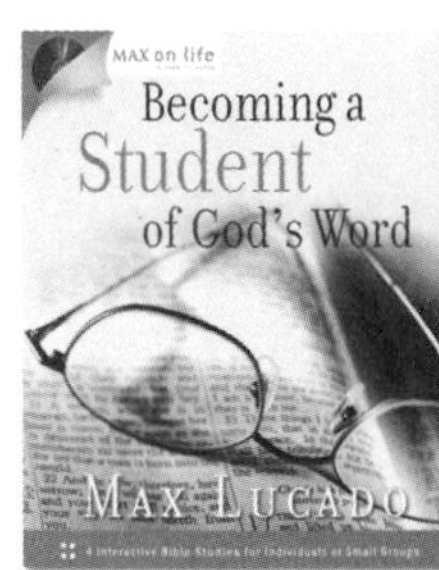

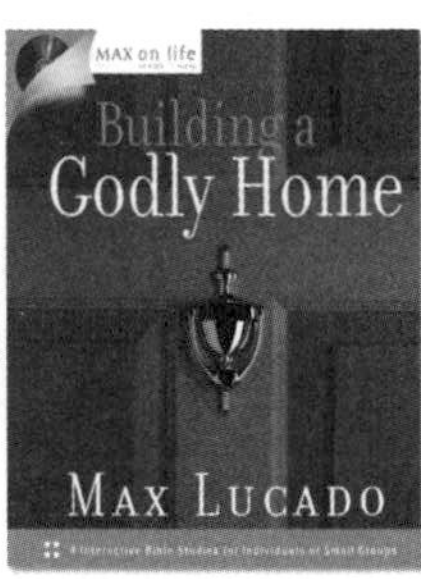

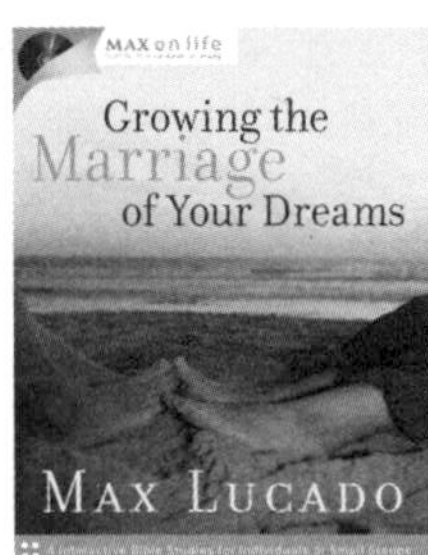

AVAILABLE WHEREVER BOOKS ARE SOLD.